I0624092

STREET SMART
CLEANUP

A BLUEPRINT FOR LITTER
MANAGEMENT ENTREPRENEURSHIP.

BY MANALOA TONATA

Copyright© 2024 Lihai Publishing

All rights reserved. No part of this book may be reproduced in any manner without the express written consent of the publisher, except in brief excerpts in critical reviews or articles. All inquiries should be addressed to Lihai Publishing.

Lihai Publishing books may be purchased in bulk at special discounts for sales promotions, corporate gifts, fundraising, or educational purposes. For details, contact Lihai Publishing at Lihaipublishing@gmail.com

Print ISBN: 979-8-9906289-0-8

Ebook ISBN: 979-8-9906289-1-5

Printed in the United States of America.

Table of Contents

INTRODUCTION

"Protecting our environment isn't a choice; it's a responsibility we owe to future generations." - ChatGPT

In today's uncertain and unstable economy, many people are feeling the same about their finances. Many individuals, perhaps even yourself, are seeking an alternative way to make money. It comes as no surprise that raising a family on one income is nearly impossible, and American families are struggling to provide basic needs, even with two incomes. This is causing many to rethink their financial paths and look for alternative sources of income to supplement their jobs or replace unreliable employment altogether. As many businesses face challenges such as labor shortages, wage demands, and societal issues like homelessness and drug use, the need for fresh solutions arise. This how-to-guide presents the opportunity for readers to be one of these solutions and change their current financial situations. By delving into the complexity of building and running a litter management business while reading this book, readers gain access to valuable resources, updated advice, and proven strategies to guide them through this tedious yet rewarding process.

Within the pages of this guide, aspiring entrepreneurs interested in starting a litter management business will discover a toolkit filled with important advice and resources along with customizable forms to help streamline day-to-day operations. This toolkit also includes savvy tips on how to effectively market and brand your business while simultaneously building an online community. Having the necessary tools to get the job done right is only half of the equation. You will need a blueprint to show you where to start and help you progress through the process. Let the chapters in this book be that blueprint. Each chapter tackles common hurdles and unforeseen circumstances. Be sure to utilize the blank lined pages at the back of this book to take notes as you progress. By using these tools and the blueprint provided, I hope you will have the faith to take your first step toward financial freedom through building your own litter management business.

ABOUT THE AUTHOR

Manaloa Tonata is a hard-working and dedicated family man who recently moved to Nevada with his wife and two young boys. Mana's background is rooted in blue-collar work, having spent his life in hands-on labor as he grew up on a ranch alongside his little brother Joey and other siblings. Mana learned the values of hard work and discipline from an early age. With a deep faith in God and unwavering conviction, Mana is a man who finds strength in his beliefs and faces challenges head-on. Mana hopes to inspire others to pursue their dreams with courage and determination. Knowing that with hard work and faith, anything is possible.

A WORD FROM THE AUTHOR

I started this business because I wanted to maintain my full-time job at the time, which provided valuable experience and good pay. Additionally, during the COVID-19 pandemic, I was deemed an essential worker and remained employed throughout the crisis. However, I also desired to explore entrepreneurship without the financial burden of hefty startup costs and ongoing monthly expenses, especially if no income was being generated at the beginning. I sought out a business venture that offered flexibility, allowing me to build and maintain it alongside my full-time job.

Starting a litter management business checked both of those boxes for me. It provided the opportunity to dip my toes into entrepreneurship without substantial upfront investments or costly fixed monthly overhead. This business has opened avenues of opportunity that I never previously considered. Looking back on where I stand today, I can confidently say that it was a wise decision. The business experience I have gained thus far has been invaluable, shaping my understanding of how business is conducted and equipping me with knowledge that will stay with me for a lifetime. This, too, is what I hope for you, my friend.

- Manaloa Tonata

A SPECIAL THANK YOU

My parents, who taught me how to work hard; my siblings, who worked hard with me growing up; my wife and kids, who will continue to work hard with me for the years to come. Finally, to God for... everything

Thank You!!!

CHAPTER 1

Businesses Need Outsourcing

"The Earth is not just our home; it's a shared sanctuary. Let's treat it with the respect and care it deserves." - ChatGPT

In this section, we will be focusing on why there is a growing need for businesses to outsource daily operational duties to contractors like me and so many others around the world, starting with the cost-saving benefits that outsourcing offers. Outsourcing presents a cost-effective alternative to traditional employment models. This is one of my favorite topics to discuss with businesses because the thought of reducing overhead expenses is so appealing. I include these exact examples in my advertising and presentations, which often get the prospects' inner gears running, and sometimes I can even see it on their faces.

One such benefit is eliminating the need for businesses to match payroll taxes for health insurance, retirement, and government/state taxes as they would with an employee. Moreover, there are no costly long-term commitments or extensive training requirements associated with outsourcing, which reduces the financial burdens on businesses. When you compare hiring a full-time employee, a sweeper company, or a landscaper with an outsourced independent contractor, outsourcing proves to be a more economical option. Additionally, outsourcing services provide flexibility and efficiency and demonstrate a commitment to cost-effectiveness in daily operations. Outsourcing to independent contractors gives a business a competitive edge by optimizing resources and maximizing R.O.I. (return on investment). This need will only grow in the years to come.

Benefits for businesses that hire *you*

Now that we have discussed the cost-saving benefits of hiring contractors, let's highlight what you can offer businesses as a litter management service provider. Several key advantages emerge when considering outsourcing to you versus a sweeping company or a full-time employee. Firstly, businesses stand to benefit from lower employee overhead costs because independent contractors are self-employed, thereby alleviating the need for employee benefits and payroll taxes. Secondly, contractors specializing in litter management tend to be more detail-oriented and invested in their work. As they take pride in being owners of their businesses, this sense of ownership translates to a higher level of commitment to delivering quality service.

How so? Consider it like this: businesses gain the advantage of having an extra set of vigilant eyes on their property as contractors actively look out for issues like graffiti, vandalism, or abandoned property. They contribute to enhanced security and maintenance efforts, and you will want to highlight this benefit to the client during the quoting process. Finally, another thing businesses need to consider is the rise in public drug use in today's environment. These hazards, like fentanyl, pose serious risks and businesses can benefit from hiring contractors who prioritize safety and are equipped with the necessary protective gear and training to handle potential dangers. The use of puncture-proof gloves and specialized tools minimizes exposure to harmful substances. This benefits the client by providing a safe and secure environment not only for themselves but for their customers as well.

CHAPTER 2

Business Planning

"In the symphony of nature, let our actions play the harmonious tune of cleanliness and preservation." - ChatGPT

This might be slightly different from what you're used to hearing. To tell you the truth, it doesn't feel very pleasant even saying it aloud, but I think this business model is an exception. What are these mystery words? I don't want you to focus on an overly detailed business plan. Yes, I said it.

If you still can't believe it, let me say it in another way. I don't want you to prioritize or create an excessively detailed business plan. I mean this so intently that I have the simple business plan—one which I used myself—for you to download on our website under forms. I say this because, luckily for you, service-based businesses are typically cheaper and easier to start than product-based businesses. Even luckier for you, I have taken half of the work off your hands by giving you a business plan that you can tweak with your specific details. You can also find marketing flyers, W9s, and operational forms (property assessment reports, campaign forms, property surveys, invoices, and proposal forms). I even give you proven phone scripts, voicemail script, and an e-mail script, all of which can be downloaded for free via PDF from our website www.lihaipublishing.com.

Now, like any book you read on building a business, the first informative chapter is on actually planning out the business itself. And well, you can't dive into the subject about business planning without talking about the big scary business plan monster. A few times, I've wondered how many dreams the business-plan monster has gobbled up. All those people with great ideas, inventions, or innovative products cooked up in their minds. Perhaps they even wrote down their good ideas only to immediately be met with the rigorous and tiring task of making a business plan.

CHAPTER 3

Services Offered

"Every act of cleaning up is a love letter to Mother Earth, expressing gratitude for the life she sustains." - ChatGPT

Detail the range of litter control services your business will offer and what areas of the property will be under your care. I advise you to stick with the following when getting started:

Exterior litter/trash pick-up (sidewalks, landscape, courtyards, and parking lots)

- Dumpster area clean-up
- Exterior trash can liner swap out
- Gutter sweep out
- Doggy parks clean up
- Property assessment report (see inspecting and reporting sections)

Perhaps you'll decide to offer more services, or customize services for a specific customer in time. Such services may include:

- Seasonal promotions/specials
- Rake leaves/leaf blower
- Shovel snow/salt walkways
- Graffiti removal

- Interior litter/trash pick-up (i.e., apartment hallways, gyms, break rooms, cafeterias, etc.)

Remember to listen to your client's needs and ask questions if you are still unclear. Do not be afraid to stay firm on the types of services you ultimately choose to offer. I promise you the more clients you get, the more likely you'll run into someone who will try to get you to do more than you agreed to in your contract. This someone might not even know what you contractually agreed to because they may be an employee of the business or a maintenance guy who wasn't present during the discussion or the contract signing. This is one reason why we keep and document the contracts we sign.

Inspecting and Reporting

One service that I know is attractive to possible clients is the property assessment reports (see picture in Chapter 9). This form will indicate any damage or vandalization to buildings, parking covers, fences, sidewalks, or roads. You may also record burned-out light bulbs, suspicious activities, or broken and abandoned cars. All of these should be reported to the appropriate person immediately and written down under notes in the property assessment report. There are also columns to document the date and time of service, how many bags were used, and how much the job cost.

Nowadays, most businesses, apartments, and warehouses have cameras, so you might as well use them to your advantage. What do I mean by this? Suppose you have a client who questions or doubts whether you showed up to do the job on a specific day. In that case, you can refer them to their security cameras with the exact time of day along with written documentation of your visit (i.e., the property assessment report).

You want to track how many bags you use from your personal stock because you will likely have clients who will need you to provide bags yourself. Then, you can get reimbursed for the bags on an invoice. This is more convenient for you or your client, especially if you perform the job after hours. Providing bags from your own stock is perfectly fine. In the bag use tracking column on the form, you can record the number of bags used for each job, simplifying the process across multiple properties.

You can use bags from a single box rather than allocating a separate box for each property. For instance, if a box contains 30 bags and you use 10 bags for property A, 15 bags for property B, and 5 bags for property C, all bags will be accounted for. When it comes to invoicing, the process is equally straightforward. When a customer uses an entire box of 30 bags (perhaps over a span of several months), then you can charge them on the next invoice. This ensures a transparent and efficient billing process.

Note: Always provide a copy of the property assessment report to include with the invoice when submitting to the client each month. Keep the originals in your business files.

Your Services vs Sweeping Companies

When I lived in Utah, one of my first jobs after moving was for a sweeping company. I drove a big yellow sweeper that had two engines—one I sat directly on—and a 50-gallon water tank. The terrible part is it had no shocks, and you can guess the number that did on my back when

I went down the freeway. The most outrageous part, though, was their prices. Because it was my job to have a representative sign them, I saw all the invoices for the customers I serviced on behalf of the sweeping company. The lowest price we offered was $100 an hour, which did not include trash/litter clean-up for sidewalks, landscaping areas, or trash can liner swaps. On top of that, if an item was too big to sweep up or something was in the way, we would go around it. Sounds like a lot of money for a lot of nothing.

I use these facts in my marketing efforts. This could be mentioning it in a flyer or incorporating it into my phone script as a response to "We already use a sweeping company for this type of service." In my experience, sweeper businesses will be your main competition, but their expensive costs create an opportunity. Will you be the solution?

The value of "recurring" jobs

The primary objective is to provide consistent long-term property litter management for each client, whether the client has one or multiple properties. Getting these types of contracts presents a valuable opportunity for steady revenue. Unlike one-time jobs that offer intermittent income, consistent jobs offer a reliable income stream for your business. This helps provide stability and predictability, which are both particularly important for the growth of a new business. Overall, consistent jobs will be a cornerstone of substantial growth and success for your litter cleanup business. It will offer stability, reliability, and opportunities for long-term profitability.

The value of "one-time" jobs

One-time jobs provide a means of diversifying your revenue streams, reducing your dependence on contractual sources of income. Offering one-time jobs also offer flexibility and customization and allows clients to request your services without committing to long-term contracts. If a business requests services you usually don't provide but have the skill to do so, you can be more open to this because there will be no commitment to ongoing services. Be upfront with your client about this in case they do end up wanting your services regularly.

Completing one-time jobs provides an opportunity to show off your skills and quality of work professionally. Leaving a satisfied customer in your wake can lead to referrals and possibly long-term partnerships with a business. Offering these types of jobs can also serve as an entry point to desirable customers in a different industry or niche. Again, successful jobs can lead to repeat business or referrals, contributing to the growth of your business.

Note: Remember to follow up regularly with satisfied, one-time job recipients. Doing this keeps you in mind, and they may need your services again.

CHAPTER 4

Equipment and Resources

"Littering isn't just a sign of disrespect; it's a disregard for the delicate balance of nature. Let's restore that balance, one clean-up at a time." - ChatGPT

Tools for on-site cleaning.

When it comes to onsite cleaning for a litter cleanup business, the tools needed are pretty basic but they are essential for getting the job done effectively. It all boils down to having the right arsenal of tools readily available. A simple shovel is indispensable for scooping broken glass or cleaning up large debris around dumpsters. Additionally, a trash grabber combined with a 5-gallon bucket to transport collected waste may be your weapon of choice in the battle against trash and litter, or perhaps you'll go with the old-school way of using a broom and stand-up dustpan. Of course, no clean-up business is complete without an ample supply of trash bags. For most people, some or all these items may already be sitting around in your garage or house. These basic tools enable you to tackle litter clean-up tasks more efficiently and leave the areas spotless. Below, I have listed the tools you will need before starting your first job.

- Grabber
- Bucket
- Broom (kitchen and industrial)
- Dustpan (stand up)
- Snow shovel/Flathead shovel
- Trash bags

Safety gear and personal protectio equipment (P.P.E.)

Ensuring your safety during day-to-day clean-up operations is paramount, especially with the unique risks and challenges America has been presented with over the few years. With the rise of the homeless crisis in many cities across America combined with the increase of fentanyl and other drugs flooding our communities' public spaces, the need for proper safety gear and P.P.E. cannot be overstated. Puncture-proof gloves protect against sharp objects like needles and potentially contaminated materials. Using them reduces the risk of coming in direct contact with a harmful substance. Sturdy boots offer stability and support on uneven terrain, helping you prevent slips and falls (I prefer muck boots). Also, using high-visibility vests ensures you remain visible to traffic and pedestrians, particularly in urban areas with heavy traffic. Wearing your P.P.E. every day can mitigate potential hazards while performing litter maintenance duties. Below is a list of the essential P.P.E. items you'll need before picking up that first piece of trash.

- Gloves (Bulk)
- Boots

- High visibility vests
- Mask (optional)

Office

A home office can offer many benefits for entrepreneurs and small business owners, but one of the most notable advantages is tax benefits. By designating a portion of your home as a dedicated workspace, you may be eligible to claim tax deductions for various expenses such as property taxes, mortgage interest, maintenance, and more. Visit the IRS website at www.irs.gov and type "office in the home, frequently asked questions" into the search bar for further requirements to qualify you as a legit home office.

Now, let's say a home office for you isn't feasible at the moment. Local libraries are an excellent alternative for office space. In fact, I myself did not have the luxury of a home office, and with two toddlers, the luxury of quiet time was not an option either. Libraries offer a quiet environment, study rooms, and access to computers and Wi-Fi. My library even gave me a $5 credit to use at their printer each month. Each black and white copy costs $0.10, which is 50 marketing fliers for free. This option allows you to enjoy a dedicated office space without the overhead costs. Whichever option you choose, having a dedicated working area has been proven to enhance productivity and focus. Trust me, your business's growth and ultimate success will depend on how focused you are on your responsibilities as the owner.

Here is a list of basic supplies to consider for your office space:

- Essentials (pens, paper, index cards, stapler, file folders)

- Planner
- Filing box (I recommend a hard box)
- Presentation folder
- Stamps (I recommend buying in bulk)
- Envelopes

Transportation

Having a reliable vehicle is essential for running a litter cleanup business. Your vehicle will be the backbone of your operation, transporting you and your tools from property to property each day. Many people assume that a truck is the only suitable option for this line of work, but I have found in my own experience that a small compact car can be just as efficient, if not better. We all remember the high gasoline and diesel prices during and after the COVID-19 pandemic. Another way to look at it is if you don't have a truck, you won't be the one friends call to help them move. This is the option I went with. I used a 2004 Toyota Corolla at the start of my business and still use it today (see picture). This bad boy gets me everywhere with minimum repairs and good fuel efficiency. Plus, I only paid $2000 for it. It is by far the best investment I made for the business, leading me to the next transportation topic.

Using a hoopty vehicle for your business

Consider this next paragraph an opinion piece—food for thought, if you will. I want to mention the benefits of using a hoopty car because, as entrepreneurs, we must put the needs of our business before our own egotistical desires. The humility we experience along this journey only serves to humble us. What is a "hoopty car"? The best way I can explain it is it's a vehicle that's older and well-used. Perhaps this will be evident in the exterior or interior cosmetics, although there are plenty of nice-looking beater vehicles out there. One of the two main benefits I will discuss is reduced overhead expenses. By going with an older vehicle, your insurance premium will usually be cheaper, registration will be less expensive, and if you paid cash, then there will be no monthly payments. All of this helps you save money, freeing up funds to invest in other areas of your business.

The second benefit is reduced stress. With a beater vehicle, wear and tear from daily operations is less concerning. Scratches, dents, and other minor damages from transporting tools are par for the course, but with a hoopty vehicle, there's no need to worry about maintaining a pristine exterior. This peace of mind allows you to focus on the task at hand without the added stress of potential vehicle damage.

Resources

Below is a list of some resources you might want to consider:

Mileage tracker: A mileage tracker app conveniently and accurately tracks and records miles driven for business-related trips. Tracking your miles is essential for tax deductions, expense reimbursement, and operational costs.

Microsoft 365: Microsoft 365 played a pivotal role in the operations of my litter cleanup business. With its many tools and applications, doing even the most mundane administration tasks are easier and streamlined. Tasks like creating and editing flyers, invoice templates, phone scripts, e-mail scripts, proposals, and much more are all on one platform. Don't forget that this expense is a tax write-off as well.

Business insurance: Business insurance is critical for any small business, including a litter cleanup business. It provides financial protection and peace of mind in the case of unforeseen events or liabilities. Luckily, because a litter clean-up business does not involve high-risk activities—like using heavy equipment or power tools—my insurance premium is the lowest they offer. Business insurance is essential for the risk associated with cleaning public spaces and interacting with the public. The most common insurance packages cover you and your business in case of property damage, bodily injury, or legal claims. As the adage goes: "Better to have it and not need it than to need it and not have it."

Forms: In the day-to-day operations of your litter cleanup business, having well-designed forms is crucial for smooth communication, organization, and record keeping. These tools are used to collect essential information, document agreements, market your business, and help with daily operations. Below, you will find a comprehensive list of forms you are more than welcome to use in your litter cleanup business. All these forms can be found and downloaded free from our website at www.lihaipublishing.com. You will also see pictures of most of them in Chapter 9.

Property Assessment Report
- Campaign Form
- Proposal Form
- Property Survey Form
- Promotional Fliers
- Invoice Form
- IRS W-9 Form

CHAPTER 5

Marketing and Branding

"Beneath the weight of scattered waste, our planet cries for gentle hands to cleanse its face." – ChatGPT

In this chapter, I'll talk about my approach to keeping potential leads organized using the campaign form. The campaign form (see picture in Chapter 9) is a practical tool for maintaining order for potential leads and customers, featuring important columns like company name, property type, phone number, address, and notes. It serves as a structured road map along with checkboxes to indicate lead status. This form is not just about recording information but about avoiding overwhelm. Businesses gain a clear and organized view by systematically documenting details and categorizing leads as uninterested, unreachable, or undecided. This form is a straightforward tool that prevents chaos by helping you navigate through leads efficiently and make informed decisions without drowning in information overload.

The campaign form is best used to target specific industry sectors like hotels, car dealerships, or apartment complexes (see more examples at the end of this section). Using RV parks as an example, I will look up all the RV parks in my county or zip code. After filling in the park's information on the form (i.e., phone number, address, name, etc.), I will start at the top of the list and call each one. Don't worry if one doesn't answer. Simply move on to the next and backtrack after completing the list. Be sure to utilize the "lead status" column on the form to indicate whether you need to follow up with any of the leads on the list.

Call it O.C.D. if you want, but I refuse to move on to another zip code or campaign until I've determined all the leads' statuses and I've followed up with the necessary ones. This, too, reduces being overwhelmed.

Other examples of possible campaigns in your area:
- Dealerships
- Apartment complexes
- Property management companies
- Car washes
- Truck stops
- Holiday events (by month)
- Hotels and motels
- REMAX offices/agents

Be creative to find other untapped niches in your area.

My approach when marketing to property management companies

Step (1) Using a campaign form, list as many property management companies in your county as possible. There is no need to try to sort out which company only manages commercial properties or which only manages residential properties. This would be futile and time-consuming.

Not only do most property management companies manage both types of properties, but you'll find this formation out in the next step.

Step (2) Now that you've got your list, call each one. Feel free to use the script I provide in Chapter 9. The main question you want to ask is: "Who manages your vendor's lists?" In most cases, this question will get you an e-mail to send your marketing flyer to (see marketing flyers in Chapter 9). This is where you ask the person on the phone, whether it be a secretary or agent, what types of property their company manages. Go ahead and send your marketing e-mail to the address provided, and be sure to keep a record of the e-mail address on the campaign form.

Step (3) In this step, we will dig even deeper into each company, but unlike steps 1 and 2, we will focus on one company at a time. I recommend you do not move on until you've completed the research for that company. This is particularly important so as not to overwhelm yourself. Starting at the top of your campaign list, type the first company's name into Google Maps. Why Google Maps? Google Maps usually gives you the address, phone number, and a link to the company's website on one page. It is essential to write down the company's address because you will need it in the next step, so save yourself time and write it down while you have it up on Google Maps. Afterward, click on the website link. The goal here is to see if the company lists its agents on its website by name. I have found that at least 50% of property management companies do list their agents by name. You can usually find this information under the "About Us" or "Our Team" tab on the company's website, which is usually a list of the company staff along with their position in the company (i.e., CEO, sales associate, agent, secretary, etc.). Remember, we are only interested in the agents in the company. There is also usually a picture that comes along with the team members' info. If you are lucky, an e-mail address for each agent will also be included. If an e-mail address for the agent is included, take the time to e-mail each agent a small message (see e-mail script in Chapter 9) and a marketing flyer. Afterward, for each agent, write down their name, company name, email address, and phone number on the campaign form.

Step (4) In this step, there are two possible scenarios. Either the company's website listed the agents by name, or they didn't. Let's investigate both.

The company did list agents by name

With the list of agents and the company's address in hand, you will make separate envelopes for each agent with the company's address on them. In the envelope include (1) marketing flyer and (1) business card. If you have some kind of promotion or discount, add that too. The goal of sending a marketing envelope to each agent is to get maximum recognition from that company. Be sure to mail them out separately. Instead of sending all the envelopes for one company at once and them possibly receiving all of them at once, try sending a few at a time throughout the week. You can send them out in batches each day with a mix of other property management company letters.

The company's website did not list agents by name

This scenario involves much less work. For example, in the previous paragraph, you would be sending multiple envelopes to one company, whereas in this scenario, you'll only be sending one. That one envelope will have the company's address, and I like to address it to "Vendor Support." Finish it up with your business information in the top left corner, add your flier and business card and voila, you're done with this step.

I cannot stress how important it is to keep all the information for each company organized and readily available. Why? Because you will be doing steps 2 and 4 every three months or when you have a new promotion. The only difference is in Step 2, you will not need to call the company again. You saved the e-mail address they gave you the first time, so send a marketing flyer or promotion to this same e-mail.

Marketing to strip malls, industrial business parks, commercial office buildings, and vacant lots

In this section, I will provide you with a special formula to help you find the correct owner of a business, vacant lot, or building. This can be an individual, corporate company, real estate company, or even the exact property management company in charge of overseeing a specific property you are pursuing. This formula could be used by most businesses offering services. On top of that, I have never seen this taught anywhere else. You will have a leg up on the competition right out of the gate. I can't promise this formula can be applied in every county in America, but I know it can be widely used because it is a government resource. Most county websites are similar in terms of tools and research capabilities. This formula is used after the first two steps have been taken. It is more like a last-ditch effort. With that being said, let's get started with the first step.

Step (1) This step may be obvious, so bear with me. You'll first want to call the businesses associated with the property in question and see if they know or can find out who's picking up the trash/garbage in the parking lot. However you ask this question is totally up to you. Remember, most often, in the case of strip malls, corporate industrial parks, and commercial office buildings, these are not the ones you want to pitch your business to. It is strictly an information-gathering call. Also, I like to ask for a manager because they are more aware and probably have been with the company for a while. I like starting with this step because it is faster and cheaper than the next one.

Step (2) Ok, so maybe you didn't have any luck with Step 1. That's fine. We still have a few tricks up our sleeves. Next, you will want to visit the location of the property you are interested in putting in a bid on. Once there, look for signs or banners with leasing information, such as a real estate or property management company name and a phone number for people who are interested in leasing space. Sometimes, this will not be available for non-vacant properties/buildings. Also, sometimes this step is easier to get the correct information the first time than Step 1. I only make it Step 2 because it takes time and money to travel to each location.

Step (3) This step is the most complicated as it involves using a smartphone, tablet, or computer. Here, you will be introduced to the formula previously mentioned.

Formula:

$$\frac{\text{Property}}{\text{Address}} + \frac{\text{Parcel}}{\text{Viewer}} = \frac{\text{Owner}}{\text{Managing company}} + \frac{\text{google}}{\text{County Business Records}} = \frac{\text{Contact Info}}{\text{to Pitch Proposal}}$$

Formula breakdown:

Once you have the address for the property you want to place a bid on, you'll be ready to start the process. Next, you will want to use the address to get the parcel details via your county's parcel viewer map. Typically, it is the responsibility of the county government or a specific department within the county government to keep records and manage parcel data.

What is a parcel? A parcel refers to a piece of land or real estate that has been defined by boundaries (which shows you exactly how big the property is), who can own it, and what it can be used for. That said, you will first want to go to your county government website. It may take time to find the interactive parcel map. You could call the county office and ask for step-by-step instructions on finding this. This tool is often referred to as Geographic Information Systems (G.I.S.) so watch for this abbreviation while researching your county website.

Once you find the parcel map, type the property address into the search bar. This will bring up said property along with some limited information. It will also include a link to see parcel details. Clicking on this link will give you everything about the property, such as location, ownership, ownership history, description, appraisal, classification, assessed value, taxable value, and all documents related to the property. You are only interested in parcel ownership as this tells you who or what owns the property. This generally will be an individual person, LLC, investment company, or real estate company. I have sometimes even been lucky enough that it includes the property management company as a reference contact, although this is rarely the case.

In the case the owner is an individual, which is usually the case for a vacant lot, you can use the web or social media to find the individual. Honestly, I only reach out to individual people for vacant lots or abandoned businesses. In the situation of strip malls, industrial business parks, and commercial office buildings, the individual owner tends to have nothing to do with everyday operations, so contacting this person seems unprofessional, but it's your business/brand to run as you wish. If the owner is an LLC, real estate company, or investment company, this is where the next part of the formula comes in.

Before moving on, let's recap. So far, you've obtained the property address that you're interested in. Then, by searching the address on the parcel viewer map on your county government website, you know who owns the property/business. Again, generally, this would be an individual person, LLC, investment company, real estate company, or property management company. Great, let's continue.

Now armed with the name of the company or LLC that owns the property, you can use the county website again to look up the business information under the business records section of the website. After typing the name of the company or LLC into the search bar, you will get the exact information you are looking for, including company address, phone number, business owner, and much more. You will use this info to either pitch your business to or ask who is managing this property for them. Feel free to tell them straight up that you are interested in putting a bid in for litter cleanup for their property. Doing so might calm any worries they may have. They may be wondering why this person is asking about their company's assets. If the county website is too much for you to navigate, you can generally get the same results by typing the company or LLC that owns the property into Google Search.

My approach when marketing to all other property types listed in "Campaign Examples"

Regarding the other examples I give under campaign examples, these types of businesses are relatively easy when figuring out who to pitch your business to. Simply call the place of business and ask to speak to the manager since the managers at these types of businesses run the day-to-day operations. Sometimes, you may be transferred to a maintenance department, but with most businesses, you'll be pitching to the manager. It is important not to pressure the manager to make a decision on the spot. Just convey to them what you do and that you're looking to send them a flyer with more information via e-mail. Doing this puts them at ease, and often, they'll gladly give you an e-mail address. Instead of puking a bunch of information about your business over the phone and expecting them to digest it all at once (which is not an effective approach), let your business flyer speak for you. Feel free to leave a voicemail if there is no answer (see voicemail script in Chapter 9) but be sure to document everything on the campaign form. After your initial marketing email, send another one every three months or when you have a promotion that they qualify for. You want to ensure that if they ever look outside one day and see trash everywhere, you will immediately be who they think of. It's all about getting your brand into your community.

My approach when marketing to local event organizers

Another great source of income is through local events organized by non-government entities. Some of the most common types of groups that put on these local events include, but are not limited to, community groups, local businesses, nonprofit organizations, event planning companies, and cultural associations. Keep an eye out for events such as festivals, farmers' markets, charity runs, cultural celebrations, and so much more. The best part is that social media is almost always used to promote these events, and you can find multiple leads on Facebook, X platform, snap map on Snapchat, and, well, you get the point. They're not hard to find. Even better, these platforms typically show you who is hosting the event and how to contact them. I have personally used these leads to land contracts and additional work. Most of these events can last five hours or more and usually require more than one person to complete the job, depending on how big the event will be. So, be ready to adjust your schedule if you do land a contract and have a list of trustworthy friends and family to recruit.

The significance of the term "Vendor"

In business, the term vendor refers to an individual or company that provides goods, services, or a solution to another entity, often on a contractual basis. Vendors play a crucial role in the supply chain, offering products or services that contribute to the operations and objectives of their clients.

Using the term vendor when trying to find the right party to pitch your business to helps because most people are familiar with this term. Often, companies have a specific department that manages vendors, such as the sales and purchasing departments. The term vendor is universal in most industries, and a vendor is exactly what you'd be.

My approach to branding online

As we start with the branding section of this chapter, I will be the first to admit that it will be much shorter than it should be, but it is important to acknowledge my own experience and limitations. While my experience is mostly with paid advertisements on Facebook for promoting my brand online (which will be what I touch on here), I do recognize the vast landscape of other social media platforms such as Instagram, Twitter (now known as X), and Snapchat that can be tools in your promotion efforts.

To some people, what I cover in this section will sound like basic information. Honestly, you may very well have ten times more experience and knowledge than I do. I'm not too proud of a man to admit this. If you have limitations in this field, like I did, there are plenty of free online resources at your fingertips. I would recommend starting with YouTube videos, which are an excellent resource for anything you need help developing. I have personally watched videos on marketing, cold calls, motivation, how to give a presentation, and so much more. Hell, I even replaced a carburetor and primer bulb on my snow blower after watching a 20-minute video on YouTube. It's also an excellent time to start personal self-development if you aren't already. YouTube is a great place to start for that too.

Facebook. As mentioned above, Facebook is about the extent of my social media branding experience. In my personal life, I practice simplicity, so naturally, I try to incorporate this virtue into my business. I only chose Facebook as a branding platform because it is the social media giant that I am most familiar with. In trying to keep my business as simple to operate as possible, I decided it would be more efficient and easier to channel my energy toward a single social media platform to promote my brand. Doing this ensures that while building an audience and tailoring your marketing ads, you can pour your energy, time, and resources into one singular project rather than be spread thin across multiple platforms, potentially diluting your efforts. Instead, use this time to craft compelling content with your creative mind.

Facebook Page. The first thing you should consider is a Facebook page for your business. This process is fast and easy thanks to Facebook's user-friendly technology. By creating a Facebook page, you are taking the first steps toward building an audience and a reputation in your community. Let this page be a representative for you and your business and a landing point for potential clients. That said, keep any content you post here professional. Ensure the content is related to your industry and brand identity, including logo and mission statement. Clearly communicate what your business offers and what sets it apart from competitors. Try to complete as much profile information as possible. Another essential strategy is implementing a consistent posting schedule to keep your audience engaged and informed. Experiment by posting a variety of content types, such as images, videos, links, and text posts. Below are examples of content I have used on my business page.

- Before and after pictures (see pictures)
- Environmental quotes and poems
- Beautiful images or paintings of nature
- Promote events (local)
- Polls/questions
- Offers
- Live videos
- Marketing materials

Facebook groups. The three Facebook tools that I mention in this section are Facebook pages, groups, and ads. The most successful one in promoting my business and acquiring clients has undoubtedly been Facebook groups in my area. Through local Facebook groups, you can create a credible and positive reputation for your business in the community. The good news is that Facebook has recently allowed you to join groups as a Facebook page rather than just as a personal account.

The types of groups you join are what's most important, and the types of groups related to your business would be:

- [Your city] contractors
- [Your city] small businesses
- [Your city] property management clubs
- [Your city] contract bidding
- [Your city] entrepreneurs

When you join a group, remember to read their rules (which are often stated very clearly when clicking on the group to join). You can always find the rules on the group's home page. I like to take screenshots on my phone and put them in a separate folder for easy access. Why is it necessary to familiarize yourself with the group's rules? This is because every administrator for the group can decide their own rules.

For instance, I have been part of groups that only allow you to promote your business on certain days of the week. Another group allows no business advertising, only posts looking for contractors, help, or quotes on a project. You are allowed to respond to these posts in the comments with your business information. Most admins take their rules very seriously and breaking them can quickly lead to you being kicked out, potentially denying you clients in your area. After joining some of your community Facebook groups, you'll want to implement the same strategy of having a consistent posting schedule as with your Facebook page.

Going back to simplicity, the easiest way to go about this is to post into the groups the same content you use for your Facebook page for business purposes. For example, say you post a quote with a picture of a beautiful meadow landscape onto your Facebook page as your regular scheduled post. You would then post the same post, quote, and image to all your groups you've joined. This will do two things. First, those who see and like the post may decide to also check out your page. You can even invite people who react to your post to visit your page, thus building an audience on your Facebook page while simultaneously promoting your brand locally. Secondly, most reputable Facebook groups have thousands of members, so when you post marketing materials like flyers, photos of your business card, specials or promotions, photos of your previous jobs, etc., you are essentially getting free advertisements to thousands of people right there in your city. This free resource cannot be overlooked or left out of your marketing plan.

To recap, the simple way to manage your content posting schedule is to use the same post for your Facebook page and all the Facebook groups your part of. Doing it this way only requires you to come up with one post per day. Of course, you can always do more if you decide this will be a major marketing avenue in your business plan.

Facebook ads. Again, in full transparency, my experience with Facebook ads is quite limited, and I have stuck to my "simplicity rule" by running the same ad repeatedly for years. I don't mind if you call me lazy. Honestly, you'd be half right, but we'll consider that a personal problem. However, I do recognize the immense potential within Facebook advertising, especially for service-based businesses like a litter clean-up business. Okay, so maybe my approach may have been straightforward, but I understand that there are vast opportunities in Facebook ads. That's why I will recommend checking out this comprehensive step-by-step tutorial on YouTube: "Facebook ads for service business" by Saenz Digital. In this video, Armando provides invaluable insight and guidance on creating compelling Facebook ads. It's a resource I found immensely helpful in creating my own Facebook ads, and I hope it can provide you with the same valuable insights.

CHAPTER 6

Pricing and Contracts

"A cleaner planet starts with the decision to take action. Be the change you wish to see in the world." - ChatGPT

Pricing

When it comes to pricing properties for a litter clean-up business, experience proves to be the best tool. Each property has its own needs and struggles, and identifying them and pointing them out during the quoting process can help close the deal. To help you with this step, which is step one of three I use, I have made a form to give you a clear understanding of the amount of work that may be required to service that particular property.

Let's move on to step one of my personal information-gathering strategy to determine a reasonable and beneficial quote for you and the client. The property survey form (see picture in Chapter 9) is a structured approach to pricing jobs by capturing details about both the company and the property to be serviced. This form includes designated lines and boxes for recording information like the company's name, address, and operating hours, along with specific property details like the number of trash cans with liners, ashtrays, nearby restaurants, or businesses that may contribute to the amount of litter and the amount of traffic by pedestrians or vehicles. By using this form to gather these details, you get a thorough assessment of the property's litter cleanup needs so you can provide a more accurate quote for pricing. I also used this form during the first initial meeting, where you'll offer the client the quote and point out all the services your business will provide. An example would be as follows: (5) trash can liners to swap out, (2) dumpsters to clean around, and (1) ashtray to empty. I will also tell them about the businesses nearby that could be adding to their litter problems, thus justifying the quote.

A property survey is typically scheduled over the phone. Doing a property survey is quite simple. Once an approved representative schedules a property survey, you'll simply show up at the scheduled time and walk around the property while filling out the form. Keep in mind while going through this step that the point is to determine the amount of work you can expect for that property. As a bonus, doing a property survey gives a sense of professionalism to your business.

Step (2) In this step, you will simply walk the property. Yes, it's as simple as it sounds and can be done simultaneously with the property survey. Start a timer as soon as you drive up to the property to start the survey. As you walk around, try to figure out the fastest walking route to take to cover the entire parking lot and landscape areas in the timeliest manner possible. Again, this step will get easier with experience as you service different property types and properties in various locations. Generally, I determine this by starting a timer when I drive up to the property to start the survey. This timer doesn't stop until you are completely done with your property survey and you have walked the entire exterior. Write this time down on the survey sheet. This will be the most important piece of data you will need to prepare a quote for the property.

Step (3) Now we get to the main point of these steps: getting a daily quote. Using the property survey (Step 1) and your walk-around time (Step 2), you will be ready to decide on a daily quote for this property. When I say daily, what I mean is the amount a client will pay each time you show up to do a litter cleanup, which, in most cases, will only be once on any given day. One thing I like to discuss with the client, with a bit of enthusiasm, is that this part of the negotiation is 100% in their control. The daily quote will be what you decide on, yet it must be reasonable. However, the customer will ultimately determine the number of days they will request your services. This is easier for the client because after you provide them with a daily quote, they can determine how many days a week of your services fit into their budget. I go about this by charging mainly for the time it takes me to walk around the property. I divided properties into four categories.

- 30 minutes or less - $15
- 30 minutes to 60 minutes - $25
- 60 minutes to 90 minutes (1 ½ hours) - $35
- 90 minutes or more – to be discussed with the client

Using the walk-around time from Step 2, determine which category the property falls into to establish a starting price. Then using the property survey form from Step 1, you can tack on any additional charges for factors like an unreasonable amount of trash can liners that need to be swapped, not enough dumpsters for the size of the property (constant overflow), or a congestion of cigarette butts on the ground around smoking spots. You can also charge more for specific services requested by the client that you usually do not offer unless the price is right. Using a systematic approach like this allows for fair and transparent pricing tailored to the unique needs of each property.

Contracts

As far as contracts go, simplicity is key, especially when you are starting off. All you need at the starting point is a simple contract between you and your client. This contract needs to include basic information such as business name, address, and contact information, along with specific terms outlining the services to be performed, frequency of service, and pricing (including a daily and monthly price). Additionally, the contract should specify how payments will be made and any penalties for past-due payments. Finally, you should include clear instructions on how either party can terminate the contract if necessary.

It is important to never start a job without both parties' mutual signing of the contract. Always have two copies of the contract, each signed by both parties. One is for your records, and the other is for your client. Furthermore, if you are offering discounts, promotions, or specials, be sure to document these in the contract, along with any expiration dates if applicable. By incorporating these elements into a simple and comprehensive contract, you and your client can navigate the business relationship with transparency and confidence.

CHAPTER 7

Extra Tips to Grow Your Business

"With every piece of litter lifted, the earth breathes a sigh of relief, whispering thanks in the rustling leaves." - ChatGPT

Marketing Mondays. Leaving Mondays open without any scheduled properties to clean provides several advantages, so keep the following in mind when picking cleaning days with the customer.

Holiday Scheduling. If a holiday falls on the same day, you will usually maintain the properties. You could utilize Monday as a regular workday and reschedule properties to this day or as needed. This helps keep your revenue consistent, and there is no need to sacrifice time with family and friends.

Severe Weather Conditions. Depending on where you live, there might be times when weather conditions like heavy rain, snow, winds, or hail prevent you from carrying out your duties for that day. By leaving Mondays open, you can reschedule properties or use it as a makeup day. This, again, minimizes the risk of lost income.

Scheduling Business Meetings. The main reason I leave Mondays free from cleaning properties is that I like to have one weekday to build and grow my business. I call them "Marketing Mondays." Use this day for meetings, cold calls, and a day to make mailers or promotional emails to send out. You can even feel free to use this day for personal appointments like for the doctor or dentist. If you have one day set aside for the above situations, you can jam-pack the rest of the week with properties to maintain.

Neighborhood Flyer Strategy. If you maintain an apartment complex or business with houses around it, consider distributing flyers to each nearby house. This can be done by mail with a modest quote. This quote could range from $5 to $10 a job, with most houses only needing around 10 minutes to do the job. Duties might include keeping the front yard, backyard, and landscaping areas free from litter/feces.

Tapping Into Teen Traffic. Here is a hot one for you. An often-overlooked niche in litter management is businesses near high schools or middle schools, and the prime types of businesses are fast food restaurants, coffee shops, pizza parlors, and recreation centers that are especially affected during lunch breaks and after school hours. Who knows, you could be the solution the business never knew existed.

Visual Marketing. When creating/designing your marketing material, consider incorporating visual images to convey what type of service you're offering clearly. Try including images such as grabbers, buckets, or someone picking up trash using a grabber, which will help differentiate your business from sweeper companies and landscapers. Just remember that you want to attract the right clientele so neither's time is wasted.

Stand Out with Laminated Flyers. When marketing to a highly desired business, try laminating your flyers to make them stand out from the jumbo mess on their desk. Laminated flyers serve two purposes: First, they make your flyer bigger than all other pieces of paper, making it noticeable amidst a cluster of other flyers. Second, they preserve the life of your flyer by preventing it from being crumbled or torn. I would suggest only doing this with specific prospects because laminating can get expensive.

Leveraging ChatGPT for Business Growth. By the time this book gets published, I expect all of you will know what ChatGPT is, but in case you don't, it is an AI language model developed by OpenAI that is capable of generating human-like text based on input prompts. This tool can be used for marketing ideas, brainstorming, cold call scripts, and lots of insightful suggestions. Simply be creative.

Include Google Maps Screenshot with E-Mail. An excellent way to avoid confusion when sending a quote via e-mail is to include a screenshot of the property from Google Maps with the area you're bidding on highlighted in blue or yellow. You can edit the screenshot in your photo app. Doing this not only gives the customer a clear scope of what they'll be paying for, but it can also potentially save you from any misunderstanding in the future should the customer sign a contract with you.

Tool Investment. When you first start, I suggest holding off on purchasing any tools you don't already have until you have secured your first signed contract. Prioritize your funds toward marketing. Remember, having shiny tools will not matter without a customer in hand.

Cost-Saving Solutions for Buying Supplies. As mentioned in the equipment and resource chapter, many of the tools and supplies used daily might already be lying around your home. For the items not at your disposal, consider buying them used or new on buying and selling apps like Facebook Marketplace or Craigslist. Also, consider buying in bulk to get the best bargain price. Some examples of items I have personally bought on these platforms are:

- Gloves (bulk/new)
- Tools (used/new)
- Stamps (bulk/new)
- Envelopes (bulk/new)
- Office supplies (bulk/new)

Professional Attire. When meeting with potential clients, it is essential to present yourself professionally. Opt for a clean, button-up shirt and work pants complemented by a reflective vest. It might even be a good idea to keep a clean pair in your work vehicle for those unscheduled meetings. For an extra polished appearance, top it off with a branded item like a hat, vest, or pens to leave a lasting impression.

Vendor Vetting Requirements: There are some businesses that I have come across that use a third party for a vendor vetting process to weed out scammers and unlicensed people. These vetting companies sometimes have strict criteria for insurance limits, vehicle insurance, and possibly umbrella insurance. If the limits are unreasonable or will eat up more revenue than it's good for, then pass and move on to another property to bid on. This process could involve a fee, so be sure to communicate with the customer that you will need to be reimbursed for it, and they will see it on the first invoice (make sure it's clearly stated on the invoice).

Leveraging Xeriscaping Trends for Business Growth. Many cities face water issues, like droughts or contaminated water, so their city governments have turned to promoting xeriscaping to conserve water. Convincing people and businesses to tear up their lawns and greenery reduces the need for lawn care and opens a niche for litter maintenance. Who will they call when they have trash in their rocks or wood chips? Not the guy with the lawnmower, but the guy with the grabber and bucket.

Capitalizing on Vacant Lots. I'm sure while driving around, you have seen vacant lots with signs that say for sale, for lease, or coming soon. Well, in this business, you can consider those money-makers. Think about it like this: the owner is trying to sell or lease the lot. Isn't it in their best interests to ensure it's clean of trash? The same goes for businesses that will be constructing or opening soon. Do they really want to enter the community with a vacant lot full of trash? Bringing these issues up with the owners could land you a contract until it's sold, or maybe longer if you can convince the new owners.

Clients in Industrial and Manufacturing Parks. Consider identifying and visiting your local industrial and manufacturing parks to find new customers for your litter management business. Look for warehouses and commercial buildings with trash in their parking lots, as these locations often have immediate cleanup needs. Using the provided phone script, call the manager of the building to bring the situation to their attention and offer your services. This could prompt immediate action from the manager. Repeat this process every few months to secure ongoing business. Another thing I like to do is encourage the manager to go out and see the trash for themselves.

CHAPTER 8

Conclusion

This book has covered various essential aspects of starting, growing, and maintaining a litter management business. We've explored practical strategies, from equipment needs and marketing to dealing with common challenges. The main takeaway is that with the right tools and mindset, you can create a successful, impactful business that not only provides financial stability but also contributes positively to the environment. By applying these insights, you're equipped to navigate this industry effectively and make a significant difference in your community.

The broader implications of this book are profound. The strategies discussed can help you not only achieve personal and financial growth but also play a vital role in addressing environmental concerns. Whether it's by keeping communities cleaner or by capitalizing on new opportunities, the lessons here can be transformative. I encourage you to take the steps outlined, experiment with the strategies, and continue learning. My personal journey in writing this book has been one of discovery and growth, and I hope it inspires you to pursue your entrepreneurial goals with confidence and determination. As you move forward, remember that every small action contributes to a larger impact, and your efforts in litter management can pave the way for a cleaner, more sustainable future.

CHAPTER 9:

Forms

Month: _____ Year: _____

Business being serviced:

_____

Contractor: _____

[Your business name]

[Your business Phone Number]

[Your business email address]

Property Assessment

Date	Time	Notes: property damage, Graffiti, abandon cars, trespassers,etc.	# of bags	Price

(_____)campaign

Date:_____   Goal:_____

                                                      _____

                                                      _____

Company address	Phone #	Notes

[Your business name]

[Your name]

[Your phone number]

[Your email address]

short staffed or can't get people to apply???

Outsource It!!! We want to take charge of all your exterior litter control needs. With a struggling workforce and higher wage demands, businesses are starting to look for ways to outsource tasks usually done by an employee. Let me make an argument for why hiring a contractor, like us, for your exterior trash clean up duties will save you money and give time back to your team to do more urgent tasks.

Who we are! [Your business name] specializes in maintaining commercial and residential properties free from all litter material. for a very economical fee of _____/day for consistent clean up or _____/one time clean up job, we'll ensure your property is free of any litter, spanning a variety of items such as plastic bags, beverage containers, food packaging, cigarette butts, and other miscellaneous debris. as well as empty outside trash cans and ashtrays. Dumpster area will be cleaned daily. We can design litter control program to meet your needs.

Why Us? Hiring us you avoid expensive long-term commitments and Paying payroll taxes, bonuses, or vacation time. Also, we are insured!!!!!! All this helping you save money and add value to your community! Please contact us. You'll find us ready and willing to help.

[Your business name here]

[Your name]

[Your phone number]

[Your email address]

short staffed or can't get people to apply???

Outsource It!!! We want to take charge of all your exterior litter control needs. With a struggling workforce and higher wage demands, businesses are starting to look for ways to outsource tasks usually done by an employee. Let me make an argument for why hiring a contractor, like us, for your exterior trash clean up duties will save you money and give time back to your team to do more urgent tasks.

Who we are! [Your business name] specializes in maintaining commercial and residential properties free from all litter material. for a very economical price we'll ensure your properties are litter free, spanning from a variety of items such as plastic bags, beverage container, food packaging, cigarette butts, and other miscellaneous debris. As well as empty outside trash cans and ashtrays. Dumpster area will be cleaned daily. We can design a litter control program to meet your needs.

Why Us? Hiring us you avoid expensive long-term commitments and paying payroll taxes, bonuses, or vacation time.

Also, we are insured!!!

All this helping you save money and add value to your community! Please contact us. You'll find us ready and willing to help.

Property Survey

Date: _____   Company: _____

Address: _____

Hours of Operations: _____   Quote for: _____

Property Type: _____   Property Size: _____

Time to Walk Parking Lot: _____   pedestrian traffic: _____

Vehicle Traffic: _____

How Many:

Description	Notes	Amount
Trash Cans		
Dumpsters		
Gutters		
Ashtrays		
Other: _____		

Nearby Businesses That May Affect Litter Amount

•	•
•	•
•	•

Visible Litter Amount: _____

Notes/Concerns:

_____

_____

_____

MARKETING SCRIPTS

Phone script:

<u>Reception/ Assistant:</u>

- Hi, my name is [**Your name**] with [**Your business name**], I'm calling hoping you'll be able to help me out, I am trying to contact who's handling the property management for your particular building.

- <u>WHY</u>? - I'm interested in putting a bid in for the parking lot litter cleanup contract.

- <u>I DON'T KNOW</u> - OK. Is there someone I can talk to that might know more please? Do you know the leasing agent?

<u>Decision Maker</u>

- Hello (Mr./Mrs.) (Last name), my name is [**Your name**]. I'm calling in regard to [**Name of building**]. My company specializes in providing parking lot litter cleanup in which we maintain your property free from all types of litter, debris, broken glass, and bigger objects. Can I ask who's responsible for your exterior litter cleanup operations for this property?

- Hi there! This is [**Your name**] from [**Your business name**]. Thanks for taking my call. I'll keep this short—I've been checking out businesses in the area, and I noticed that your parking lot and landscaping has quite a bit of trash and litter in it. Do you by chance know who is responsible for cleaning these areas? And I'm only asking because I would like to put in an offer to take care of this for your company.

Voicemail script:

- Hi, this is [**You name**] calling from [**Your Business name**], we're experts at keeping commercial and residential properties free from all types of litter and trash. we can help by taking care of your exterior trash cleanup. I would love to send over an email with more details. To discuss how we can tailor our services for you. Please call me at [**Your phone number**]. Looking forward to hearing from you!

Email Script:

Subject: Say Goodbye to Litter Hassles with [**Your business name**]!

Hi [Customer Name],

Hope you're having a great day. I wanted to introduce you to [**Your business name**], where we specialize in keeping commercial and residential exterior spaces free from all litter material. Our services are not only economical but also designed to give you back time for more urgent tasks. I've attached a flyer for your reference. I would love to discuss how we can tailor our services to meet your specific needs. Let me know when you have a moment to chat.

Thanks,

[Your Name]

[Your business name]

[Your Contact Information]

Manaloa Tonata

[Your business name]

INVOICE

[Your email address]
[Your phone number]

Bill To
[Your clients name]
[Your clients address]

Invoice #   100
Invoice Date   01/31/2024

DESCRIPTION	AMOUNT
Litter clean up (January)	500.00
Trash bags(box of 30)	15.95
TOTAL	**$515.95**

Terms & Conditions
Payment is due within 15 days
For checks make payment to:
[Your business payment info]

Powered by Invoice Home

Notes

Manaloa Tonata

Manaloa Tonata

Over the past two years, Mana has poured his heart and resources into building a litter management business from scratch. Through countless hours of hard work, including making hundreds of phone calls and delivering numerous presentations, Mana has developed his own unique formulas and strategies for success in the industry. While he may not assert himself as a seasoned professional, his commitment to sharing the most up-to-date knowledge and insights about this type of business is evident in his dedication to documenting his journey. Join Mana as he shares his experience and expertise to help others, like yourself, earn money in the litter management field.

STREET SMART
CLEANUP

US $35.99
ISBN 979-8-9906289-0-8
53599

9 798990 628908

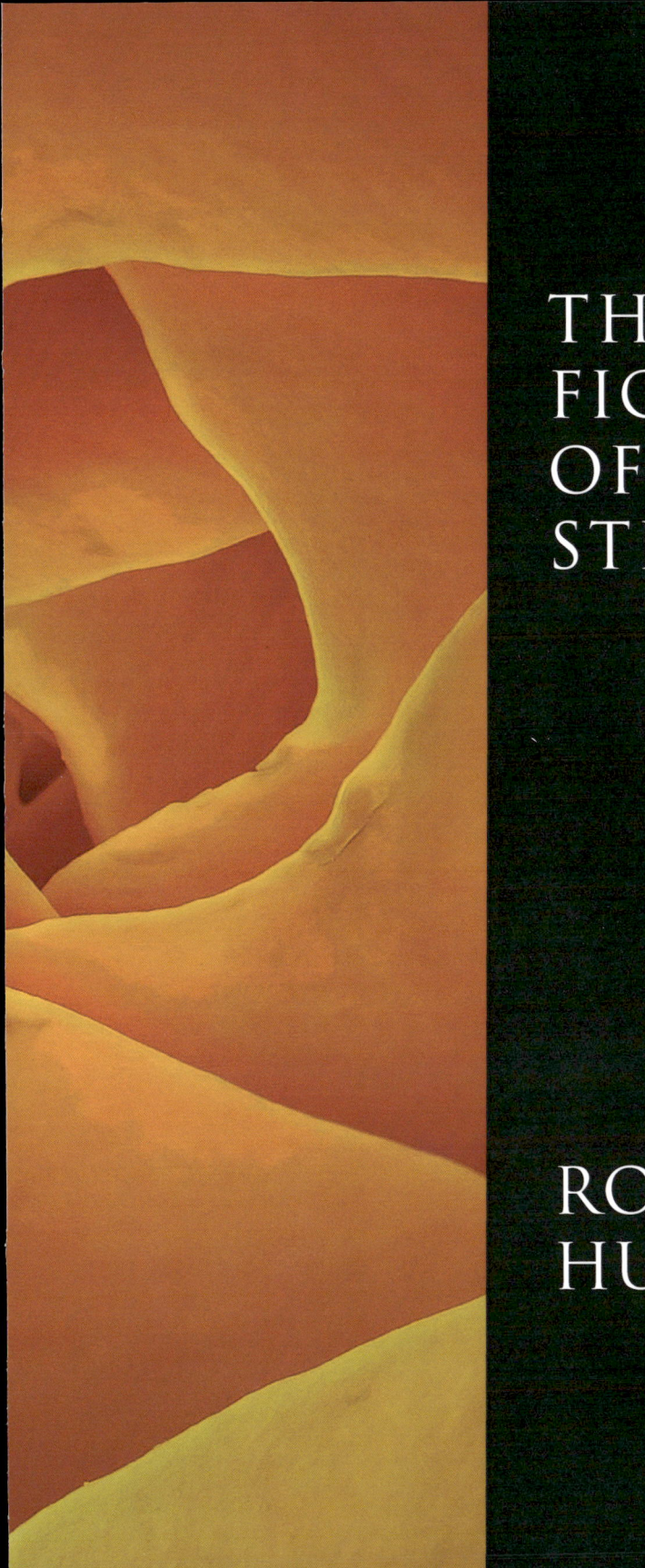

THE
FICTION
OF
STILLNESS

ROBYN
HUNT